C000221797

Gifts from the Heart of the Storm

Gifts from the Heart of the Storm

Written by

Charlie Mitchell

Illustrated by

Matthew Wiggans

First published in Great Britain in 2021 by Starseed Parenting

Copyright © 2021 by Charlie Mitchell
Illustrations by Matthew Wiggans
Formatting by The Amethyst Angel

ISBN: 978-1-7397679-1-4

First Edition

I dedicate this book to all the incredible parents with children who experience the world differently. Children with unique ways of being, with their challenges, diagnoses, illnesses, abilities and disabilities. Parents can have such different experiences ranging from crisis and feeling overwhelmed, to healing and joy. The emotions on this journey can be varied and at times feel extreme. Parents can feel isolated, with no idea who to turn to or how to manage the ups and downs.

My contact details are at the end of the story, feel free to get in touch for details of free resources and different levels of support you can access to help you on your way.

Wherever you are within your own personal storm, know that this too shall pass and you are loved, always.

Charlie

Before we Start

When we are in a challenging situation, our bodies go into flight, fight or freeze. This means we are filled with adrenaline and we are ready to act quickly as our body believes we are in an emergency situation. As parents of children with different needs, we may have been in this heightened state for some time without even really noticing.

Here are 3 things you can do right now to calm your body, no matter what else is going on:

1. Do a quick scan of your body and notice where you are feeling any tension. When you notice somewhere that is tense, clench it for a moment and then relax it as you breathe out. Start at your feet and work your up your legs, body, arms, neck and head.

2. Stand (or sit) a little straighter, with your head up and your shoulders rolled back and down. Notice how you feel a tiny bit more powerful than you did before.

3. Take a deep breath in to the count of four, hold to the count of four, breathe out to the count of four and hold to the count of four. Repeat 3 times, or as frequently as required.

These three things can take less than thirty seconds and will bring you back to this present moment, where you have a choice about how you respond and an opportunity to take a step forward, whatever is going on in your life right now.

Ideas for making this story your own

You'll find space on the pages, and even space within the pictures. Feel free to doodle, colour parts in and create pictures or symbols that are helpful on your journey. What images are meaningful for you?

Cross words out and write the words you would like to read. You can make this story even more meaningful and healing for you by adding your own words. What words would you like to read?

There are some reflective questions at the end of the story to help you with your healing journey.

Your thoughts and feelings

Free online interactive digital version of the book

You can also explore an interactive version of the book, including guided meditations and supportive questions to encourage your deeper healing:
www.starseedparenting.org/giftsbook

Denial

I slowly open one eye, uncertain what I will see,
'No, no, no, no, this is not how it's supposed to be.'
I close my eye tight shut, ignoring the raft I'm on,
'I don't want to be here, in the middle of this storm!'
I was safe and happy at home, just a moment ago
I was enjoying the sunshine – this is such a terrible blow.
'This can't be happening. I don't want it to be like this!'
I cling to my tiny raft, 'Waves, please give me a miss!'
Wind howls around me, waves crash relentlessly
'Where did my life go?' I wonder, as I look out to sea.
Bright lightning strikes nearby, and the storm rages on…

Fear

There's no let up, not even a pause, and just no relief,
I'm flung here and there by ferocious waves,
in total disbelief.
Wave after wave keeps coming, hurling me high and low,
Tossed and turned with no control,
and no choice in where I go.
I cling tightly to my raft, not sure if it will even save me,
'How could this be happening? Why won't you let me be?
What if this goes on forever? What's next?' I plead.
I can't take all this uncertainty, I can't get what I need.
I long to have a say, instead of being rigid with fear
I'm numb and overwhelmed, with confusion always here.
The waves still crash around me and the storm rages on...

What are you holding on to?

What storms are you experiencing?

Making a Deal

I don't want to be here. There must be a mistake.
I want my old life back.
Is there a different route I can take?
Maybe I can make a deal with the storm,
and promise to be good,
Perhaps I can go home soon and stay there like I should.
If I can just survive three more waves,
by clinging tightly on,
Perhaps I will magically escape and all of this will be done.
I close my eyes and hold on tight,
bracing myself ready
Yet later when I look around,
I'm still here, keeping steady.
Is this storm happening because
I've done something wrong?
What if this goes on forever?
I'm really not that strong.
The waves are just relentless as the storm rages on…

Fury

The movement of the waves seems to move my emotions
Anger starts to surge through me,
as powerful as all the oceans.
This is so infuriating!
Why won't it stop, just for a second,
So I can catch my breath?
I hate you, sea, more than I reckoned
I hate you sky. I hate you waves.
I cannot believe this is my life,
You keep on doing this to me,
and are causing me so much strife.
Moon, please stop these tides,
why did you make them start?
I'm frustrated with everything.
Why is it *my* life that falls apart?
I start to cry.
What can I do? When will this be finished?
Helplessness creeps through my veins
and I begin to feel diminished.
The ebb and flow continues as the storm rages on…

Grief

My old life feels so far away, with all the plans I had
made.
The dreams I had imagined, on the foundations I had laid.
The pain is so deep and the contrast is too much for me,
Between where I am now and where I really want to be.
I feel I have lost so much. I wish I could put things right.
One more opportunity could really change my plight.
Instead I am here alone with only my broken dreams
Wishing things were different from these painful
extremes.
Darkness is all around me and the storm rages on...

Hopelessness

No one is coming to save me.
And I cannot cope with this stress
I cannot save myself and it's all such a hopeless mess.
There's no point in trying. There's no way out of here.
I can't do anything at all. I am powerless with fear.
I am at the mercy of the storm. It must be all my fault.
Other people ride the waves, or even make them halt.
Others get out of the storm or don't have a storm at all.
If only I'd made different choices.
I feel so alone and so small.
The waves continue to taunt me and the storm rages on…

What else is getting in the way?

What is making you feel small?

What can you let go of?

What needs your love right now?

Surrender

All I can do is sink into the truth of where I'm at.
I've fought and resisted, and there's no relief in that.
Like a drop in the ocean, I suddenly feel so small,
I release my iron grip, realising I cannot force it all.
It's suddenly clear, there is nowhere else I can be
I feel pure love for all those times I tried. I see!
In this place of surrender, I sit with the joy and the pain
It's all here, allowed to be, it's deep but not a strain.
Compassion floods my being, for my steps along the way
I realise they were all needed, to bring me here today.
I'm present in this moment as the storm rages on...

A New View

From the corner of my eye, I see a new shape in the sky
A magnificent bird soaring far above the waves so high
Dominating my view with her massive, effortless wings.
We're both in the same storm,
and yet this stunning bird sings.
For a moment, I see through her eyes,
waves crashing far below
I know she can hear them, but they don't roar,
the sound is very low.
The wind, rather than being a battle, helps her to fly higher
She sees the horizon's pink glowing sunrise,
like embers of a fire.
The clarity of this wider view, the still water,
the waves cease
I see the storm won't last forever.
I feel an astonishing peace.
The things I see cannot be unseen as the storm rages on…

What If?

Knowing there is stillness out there
brings a kind of yearning
A gentle curiosity I'd not felt for so long was returning.
What if this raging storm doesn't last for all of time?
What if life is more than the storm,
a life that could be mine?
What if this raging storm is only part of the story?
What if the storm is before the calm?
Before inspiring glory?
I start to see the storm differently.
I notice the waves have gaps.
I notice a tiny shift within me,
a whisper of possibility perhaps.
Doom is a little less certain and the storm rages on…

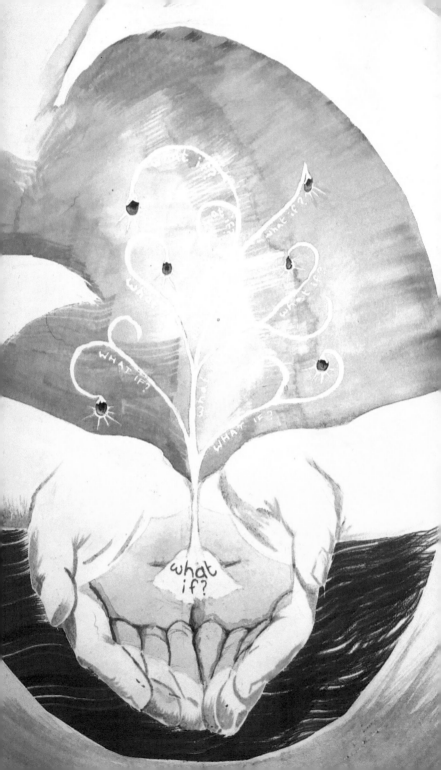

Noticing

I decide to make a little more room
for the 'what if' to grow.
What if things could improve?
Wouldn't that be great to know?
What if there are opportunities?
What if the storm's passing through?
What if my life could be different?
I would love for that to be true.
As I make room for magical what if's,
I look around and start to see
Tiny details about the waves that before had escaped me.
The waves on my left are slightly smaller
than the ones on my right
The force is a little less fierce
and it feels a little less of a fight.
I can feel movement change as I lean left
and the storm rages on…

Tiny Actions

I keep moving left and notice how the waves transform.
I see how to reach the horizon,
how to move away from the storm.
Left a bit. Straighten up. Left a little bit more.
Monumental effort, yet it feels true and pure.
I can take some action,
not just be thrown from pillar to post.
There's still so much I can't control.
Only an inch in my power at most.
A new kind of normal is emerging
from the anger and despair.
A glimpse of positivity, finding a way through feels so rare.
I take tiny actions that make a difference
as the storm rages on...

What tiny action could you take right now: look up now: what do you see?

Hope

A glimmer of hope, so small it can hardly be seen
Yet the spark has been lit and it makes me feel keen.
The glimmer of hope is there
and for the first time in a while
It has been such a long time
and it makes my heart smile.
Feeling hope, everything changes.
I can enjoy the sunrise,
The peace of stillness, and the waves,
though they're still a good size
I find the waves are not all bad:
the bright shimmer of the crest,
The deep blue murky depths
and the awe of the sea at its best.
Everything looks different in the light of hope
as the storm rages on...

Surprise

Suddenly I see a stretch of land
with a glorious beachy shore,
Much closer than I dared to dream,
I'd not seen it before
I look around and look again
as a little boat catches my eye
It's coming straight towards me,
astonished relief makes me cry
I'm greeted by singing women with smiling faces,
so kind
They gently lift me into the boat,
I can't believe this find!
They wrap me in a blanket
and pass me a hot cocoa flask
We swiftly sail back to the shore
before I have time to ask
Life changes in a moment as the storm rages on...

Friends

We arrive at a cabin on the beach,
filled with welcoming light.
'We've been waiting for you', they say,
'in this dark and stormy night.
You've been right in the eye of the storm,
a difficult place to be
We've been willing you back to the shore,
hoping you would see.
You simply couldn't see us
until you became curious and open
To possibilities, after the bird helped you
to see more options.'
I weep with enormous relief,
among friends with a thoughtful touch.
I still can't place who they are.
How do they know so much?
It nourishes my soul, that they really know
where I have been
And what it has taken for me to escape.
I feel held and seen
I settle into this sanctuary as the storm rages on…

The Next Step

After more cocoa, they explain
'This journey has another part.'
'What's that?' I ask with trepidation,
one hand on my heart.
'To look back on your journey
with the healing eyes of love.'
'There's no need.' I shake my head,
'Haven't I been through enough?'
'This deep and nourishing healing can set you free forever.
That wasn't the first time you were scared or angry ever.
By looking back with love,
you find new ways to see the past.
You can then be fully present, in this moment, here, at last.
From this fresh perspective, new opportunities appear.
You couldn't always see them and now they become clear.'
It seems my journey is not over as the storm rages on…

What do you see through your loving eyes? What else could be possible?

Exploring

'Would you like to try?' they ask.
I nervously reply, 'Alright.'
Slowly sipping my cocoa, and feeling rather uptight.
'Tell us about the storm,' they ask.
'It was tough being flung around
No time to stop or rest.
Afraid, and wishing for safe ground.'
As we sit they play calm music,
lighting a candle glowing pink.
'When was the first time you felt like that,
those emotions, do you think?'
'Hearing my parents argue, as I sat on the stairs.
I was only four.
I felt so alone, and scared.
'The memory makes my heart feel sore.
'Breathe deeply and relax,
feeling the emotions you felt back then.'
The emotions are powerful,
as I slow my breathing and count to ten.
Healing can happen unexpectedly as the storm rages on…

Softening

'Go back to those stairs, sit with her,
give her some space.
What does she need?'
'Cuddles' I reply, tears glistening on my face.
Weeping at the pain of the memory,
and the joy of belonging,
Warmth and love from the cuddle
for which I had been longing!
'You are the one you have been waiting for all this time.
You can give this loving nourishment,
helping you feel fine.
Looking back with love,
at any experience you've ever had.
You can go back to sit with that storm,
no matter how bad
Perhaps it was a long time ago,
wherever you have roamed
Each time you go back,
you bring a missing piece of you home.'
I begin to accept all my emotions as the storm rages on...

Meeting Me

'Rather than repeating negative patterns over and over
You're now free to create,
and your heart's desires come closer.'
'Can you tell me,' I ask, 'when this has worked for you?'
'Sure. My inner seven year old,
needed nourishing, she knew.
It was a difficult time when she felt desperate and alone.
Holding her, white light flowed to my heart,
changing it from stone.
Then we were in a circle with many people holding hands.
It was past, present and future versions of me
all taking a stand.
I was home.
And I finally welcomed every part of my experience.
I felt gratitude for each moment
that had given me amazing resilience.'
Unconditional love changes everything
as the storm rages on…

Courage

'No matter how tricky, challenging,
paralysing or devastating.
I felt love and compassion for each part of me
– it was breath-taking!
I have always been doing my best,
I was finally able to see.
And future me is always looking out
for past and present me.'
'So what is different now you've had this experience?'
I ask
'It has changed everything.
I am no longer scared of the past.
I know when I get upset about something,
I can mostly choose
What I will do with that emotion
– there is no win or lose.
I feel connected to the universal
and eternal nature of life
It gives my day a different perspective.
There's certainly less strife.'
Courage helps me to grow as the storm rages on...

What would be possible if you weren't scared? What helps your courage grow?

Creating Space

'I have ups and downs along the way,
but I know whatever happens
I can sit with my emotions,
I'm not wrestling demon dragons.
No matter how deep they go, how raw or how
distressing
I'm with them for as long as it takes,
I know they need expressing.
At some point, who knows when,
my emotions will heal and lift
Into something beautiful and I'll be able to see the gift.
Even if I can't see the gift right now,
I've created a safe space for me
To be with all my emotions
and it is a powerful place to be.'
I see that creating my own safe space is powerful
as the storm rages on…

Time

'I want to be there now!' I exclaim.
'Unfortunately you can't skip
From here to where you want to be
without sitting with the dip.
Your emotions need to be felt,
you need to learn to love them,
The different parts of yourself.
Sitting with pain is a rare gem –
Grief, despair, humiliation, fear, guilt, blame and shame
Joy, hope, delight, love
and others you may struggle to name.
Healing needs a little dedicated time and space to arise
A little every day and your emotional muscles
grow in size.'
I look back and see how far I've come
as the storm rages on…

How can you create space to heal? What plans can you cancel?

Resistance

'What about my children?
I want them to find healing too.
They have been through so much. What can I do?'
'Simply be a role model and show them it is possible
Give them ideas about how to heal
and show they are lovable.
I remember an experience with my son,' they say
'when I was so resistant
His leukaemia was getting me down
and the negatives were consistent.
I asked the universe for help as I went to sleep one night.
How can I get through this?
Please help me with this plight.
I saw all possibilities hanging in the air
from the worst to the best
Could I possibly sit with all of these?
It felt like an ultimate test.'
I see that being honest with myself opens my heart
as the storm rages on…

Openness

They continue 'All around me were possibilities
in rainbow colours bright
So many options were there,
and my heart opened in the light.
It felt like my resistance had been
holding back my healing
It had also reduced how present I could be for him,
was my feeling.
Connecting with all the possibilities,
I was back in the life flow
Not that this could 'save' him,
as life has its own way to go.
Knowing this liberated me to be present there with him
Fully in my personal power, full to the brim.
However things would unfold,
it felt a powerful place to be.
I could then look him in the eye and say
'You're here with me.'
Grateful for the moments we have as the storm rages on...

What helps you flow with life?

What are the other possibilities?

"we're doing this together"
"I love you
&
you're never alone."

Together

They continue 'We're doing this together.
I love you and you're never alone.'
His little body relaxed.
The importance of connection is well-known.
I knew that in that moment
so many generational patterns of pain
Were broken, as we fully connected
in the presence of now, where only love remains.
Not hiding. Not running. Not afraid.
Just accepting life right now
It's the most amazing experience
even when we don't know how.
Connection starts with our own hearts,
being our own best friend
Then we can connect with others
in ways that heal and mend.'
Together with ourselves and each other
as the storm rages on…

Full Circle

I'm grateful for their sharing,
'How do you feel about the storm now?' they ask.
'I know it is still continuing somewhere,
and I know its reach is vast
Perhaps I'll be back in the eye of the storm soon.
Yet, now I see the bigger picture,
consistent like the moon.
The storm is not the whole story.
There is more going on
I can sit with my emotions,
knowing help can arrive with a song
Who ARE you by the way?
I've been meaning to find out.'
'We are a few of the older versions of you,
emerging with some clout!
Possible options for the way the future may unfold.
We are here for you with a different view,
whatever you behold.'
Embracing every part of myself transforms my experience
of the storm raging on…

What are you grateful for?

What reminds you that you are loved?

Unconditional Love

'We are always here alongside you, offering our love
Our support you can rely on, we fit like hand in glove
However many storms come your way,
know you are not alone
You can't forget about us, now that you've been shown.
You are always loved and lovable,
and can love no matter what
Your love ripples endlessly outwards from this very spot.
Don't be afraid, you have everything you need and more
Everything is made of love
and into your open heart it'll pour.
Whatever you do, do it with love
and you'll heal many hearts.
Thank you for being you.
This is where your liberated story starts.'
I see love is all around as the storm and life flows on…

Reflections to support your unique healing journey

Spend some time sitting with different sections of the story and explore the emotions you feel.

What do you notice?

If you could get a bird's eye view of your life or the storm that is currently passing through it, what different aspects could you see?

Imagine meeting with an older version of yourself. What would this older version of you say to reassure you in your situation right now?

What is the most loving thing you can do for yourself right now?

To get access to a free interactive version of the book with more questions to support your healing visit: www.starseedparenting.org/giftsbook

About Charlie

Charlie has three incredible children who are a constant source of inspiration. They are lively, independent thinkers and each have their own unique way of being in the world. One has autism, one has both Down Syndrome and Leukaemia and the third sometimes gets caught up in the storm himself.

Charlie has had plenty of opportunities to sit with her own huge range of emotions, and uses creative self-healing approaches to help her to be the best mother she can be.

After a significant career as an Executive Coach, Charlie retrained in FreeMind Rapid Change Therapy so she can inspire as many parents as possible to take their own healing journey.

Freemind Therapy is built on the three pillars upon which success and happiness are built: peace, power and purpose. It harnesses techniques of transformation that create real and lasting change in how people are thinking, feeling and behaving.

Freemind app to support your healing

Charlie trained as a FreeMind Rapid Change Therapists because she found the FreeMind approach to be transformational in her own life, and in the lives of those who took part in FreeMind training alongside her.

The FreeMind approach and app brought a deep richness to Charlie's healing journey and inspired this story.

FreeMind combines music therapy, sound frequency, sound healing and meditation entrainment tools to make the FreeMind experience more effective, enjoyable and engaging. However, it is the unique methodology that transforms music into a healing metaphor which enables people to discover everything they need within themselves. It is the ultimate self-healing app.

Charlie regularly uses the following meditations as part of her continuing healing: sovereign surrender, support (healing), heart, past, relax, overwhelm, calm, gratitude and positivity.

The FreeMind app can be downloaded from the Apple or Android App Store.

You can find out more about FreeMind's founder, Tom Fortes Mayer and his work here: www.tomfortesmayer.com

Thank you!

Thank you for using some of your precious life energy to read this book. You can find out more about support for your healing journey on a self-study basis, in a group with other parents on a similar journey and on a one to one basis with one of our qualified therapists at www.starseedparenting.org

My dream is for as many parents as possible with children who experience the world differently to have access to this book. Please do let other parents know they can find a free online copy of the book at:
www.starseedparents.org/giftsbook